ECK WISDOM

on

Dreams

ECK WISDOM

on

Dreams

HAROLD KLEMP

ECKANKAR
Minneapolis
www.Eckankar.org

ECK Wisdom on Dreams

Copyright © 2012, 2017 ECKANKAR

The terms ECKANKAR, ECK, EK, MAHANTA, SOUL TRAVEL, and VAIRAGI, among others, are trademarks of ECKANKAR, PO Box 2000, Chanhassen, MN 55317-2000 USA.   161216

Printed in USA

Photo of Sri Harold Klemp (page 90)
by Art Galbraith

Second edition—2017

Library of Congress Cataloging-in-Publication Data

Names: Klemp, Harold, author.
Title: ECK wisdom on dreams / Harold Klemp.
Other titles: Spiritual wisdom on dreams
Description: Second [edition]. | Minneapolis : Eckankar, 2017. |
    Rev. ed. of: Spiritual wisdom on dreams. c2012.
Identifiers: LCCN 2017019600 | ISBN 9781570434471 (pbk. :
    alk. paper)
Subjects: LCSH: Eckankar (Organization)--Doctrines. | Dreams--
    Religious aspects--Eckankar (Organization)
Classification: LCC BP605.E3 S75 2017 | DDC 299/.93--dc23
    LC record available at https://lccn.loc.gov/2017019600

♾ This paper meets the requirements of ANSI/NISO Z39.48-1992 (Permanence of Paper).

CONTENTS

WELCOME TO THE REAL WORLD OF DREAMS

Why Do We Dream?

*W*hy do we dream? Why is it important to dream? Because dreaming comes from the creative imagination, which is God's gift to you and me. It is the nature of immortal Soul to dream. This is why your dreams, both in everyday life and while asleep, are so important.

Through your ability to dream, you often have experiences in the other worlds where you act as an observer. But as you move farther along, you become the participant in your dreams. You become the actor.

You begin to see goals, spiritual goals

which may be as valid as finding a home for your family. You want a place where they can be happy, a haven away from the fast pace of today's society. You create a warm place where friends are welcome.

It's a place where you can go, a home, a spiritual dream. Because as we plan our homes, whether it's a rented home or one we buy, we're just thinking of a higher home. It's the home of Soul. The place where Soul has come from, from the heart of God in the Ocean of Love and Mercy.

Dream. Dream your way home. Dream your way back to God. Use your creative imagination, because that's the only way you can return to the source of all life.

Dreams Happen in a Real World

Dreams touch every level of our life. They may let us glimpse the future, or give suggestions for healing, or share insights into our relationships. Above all, they can and will steer us more directly toward God.

What is this fantasy about dreams?

First, understand that the dream world is anything but a fantasy. A "confused" dream simply shows the inability of our mind to accept truth head-on, so it bends the facts and artfully weaves them into a story line that is less likely to cause us distress. Yes, dreams are real.

A mother listening to her young daughter tell of an inner experience from the night before dismissed it offhand as only a dream. The girl quickly corrected her. "Not just a dream, Mom," she said. "It was real."

So, first, understand that the land of dreams is an actual place. Second, any experience you gain in the dream world is as useful to you spiritually as any of those you may have here in the human body.

To grasp the universal nature of dreams, take a step back and imagine that you are standing at the top of all worlds. The identity that can do that, to command a view even of creation itself, is the real you—eternal Soul. Soul is a child of God, and, by nature, godlike. And so It can share in the divine attributes of wisdom, joy, freedom, and divine love.

So why doesn't It? Why don't you?

Your dreams are like a telescope that can give a better view of something that is normally out of reach: your spiritual side. That includes how you act, feel, reflect, think, react, and even love. Most people fear putting the telescope of dreams to their eye, afraid of what they might see.

Your Hidden Life

Dreams are a direct line to the sea of our hidden life, much like a fishing line dropped from a small boat into a bottomless sea.

A person who learns to dream well can usually take everyday life in stride, because dreams give him or her a perception that others cannot help but notice. An understanding of dreams can steady us for the surprises of the day, and so aid us in learning to manage stress with more foresight and grace.

Dreams often tell what's coming.

A friend from the air force and I keep in touch with an exchange of letters every few months.

Usually, he comes for a visit in the dream world on the inner planes while writing me a letter. Next morning, I'll tell my wife about our visit on the inner planes.

"Ray must be writing a letter again," I say.

And it usually comes a few days later.

Dreams are like that fishing line dropped from a boat into the sea. But they are much more than a communication link, which the line suggests. Our memory of dreams is a glimpse of the full spiritual life that each of us leads beyond the physical.

Our daily physical life has as little scope or variety as might exist in a rowboat. A full spiritual life, on the other hand, includes all events around the boat (human self), including those within the sea, on the land, and in the sky of existence.

Dreams are a large part of each person's hidden life, and it's this sea of experience that we want to look at.

Your Source of Everyday Guidance

Dreams can tell us everything we need to know to get along in this life. Yet how many people really believe that? If people actually did, the study of dreams would be much more prominent in our society than it is today.

Most of my life I also paid little regard to dreams.

My early dreams were of two kinds: the bad and the good. The first were nightmares, and the less they came, the better.

Even the good dreams had little to recommend them, since everything in them was topsy-turvy. I usually blessed the deep and dreamless sleep, because in that unknowing state there was a kind of refuge which did not threaten my waking life.

In fact, my recollection of dreams started to flower shortly after I began my study of Eckankar in 1967. My desire to Soul Travel had aroused my curiosity about the invisible worlds, and soon I bought a notebook to record any adventure that might occur there.

Dreams taught me to face myself, let me see the future, took me to the heavens of God, and even apprised me of impending illness and where to obtain the cure.

A Dream Guide Who Can Help You

Daydreams, night dreams, contemplation, Soul Travel—all are steps in the pursuit of heaven. In Eckankar, the student is under the protection of a spiritual guide known as the Mahanta. This is the Spiritual Traveler, the Dream Master.

As the Mahanta, he is the Inner Master. The Inner Master is not a physical being. It is someone you see in the inner planes during contemplation or in the dream state. He may look like me, he may look like another ECK Master, or he may even look the same as Christ. All it is, really, is the merging of the Light and Sound of God into a matrix, into a form which appears as a person. This, then, becomes the inner guide which steers a person through the pitfalls of karma, the troubles we make for ourselves through ignorance of the spiritual laws.

The Master often works in the dream state because it is easier to get through. Fears can inhibit and prevent one from exercising the freedom and power and wisdom which are the birthright of Soul. In the dream state, the Inner Master can begin working with

8

you to familiarize and make you comfortable with what comes on the other side.

The Living ECK Master is the other half of the title *the Mahanta, the Living ECK Master*. This means the outer spiritual teacher, myself.

Thus, the spiritual leader of Eckankar can work both inwardly and outwardly with all who come to learn of God and life.

Spiritual Exercise: The Golden Cup

Every evening at bedtime visualize a golden cup by your bed. Its beverage is your dreams. When you first awaken, in a morning contemplation, drink from this cup in your imagination. You are drinking in the night's experiences. It is a conscious way of saying, I wish to recall my night's activities on the inner planes while my body slept.

The golden cup is Soul; it is you. You are one and the same.

As you get in the habit of drinking from

9

this cup, this practice takes on a life of its own. The more the ECK (Holy Spirit) refills this cup, the more Soul (you) shines of Its own golden light. You become an ever-brighter instrument for the Holy Spirit.

Your conscious experiences, day and night, will lead to a greater understanding of your place in the spiritual order of life.

HOW TO REMEMBER AND INTERPRET YOUR DREAMS

*O*ne of the reasons I recommend keeping a dream journal is that if these inner experiences are not recorded when they happen, most of them will be forgotten. Even if an experience doesn't seem to mean much now, at some point in the future you might look back at it and recognize its spiritual significance.

Another benefit to recording your dreams is that as you study and check your dream journal, you're going to find that you remember your dreams better and better.

One of the ways to begin working out the inner tangles and knots, where the communication lines between the higher worlds and the physical have been twisted, is to work with the dream journal. And as you write, you will find that the tension in your stomach goes away. If the dream journal can help to do this, it's done something.

Dream Symbology

The real importance of dream symbology is in how it relates spiritually to your daily life. A member of Eckankar I'll call "Tim," for his privacy, discovered this through a dream about his wife, who is not in Eckankar.

In their outer life, his wife appeared somewhat interested in ECK, but she wasn't quite sure that she wanted to become a member. At various times she had also considered either staying in her present religion or looking into some other spiritual teaching. She often discussed her dilemma with her husband.

One night Tim dreamed that his wife called him at home. She said, "I'm at a phone booth, but I don't know where I am. I'm lost. Can you help me get home?"

"If you know the name of the road you're on, or even a nearby crossroad, I can help you find your way home," Tim said.

"There aren't any crossroads around here," she said. "I don't know where I am."

"OK, get in the car and drive down the street very slowly until you come to an intersection. Then call me back and tell me the names of the two crossroads. We'll be able to figure out where you are."

Tim woke up wondering what the dream was all about. The experience on the inner planes had been so lifelike that he knew it was trying to tell him something.

Suddenly he realized it was an answer to his fear that he may have been pushing Eckankar on his wife. At times he thought she seemed truly interested in the teachings of the Holy Spirit. But he had often wondered, *Does she really care, or am I only imagining her interest?*

The dream had given him a spiritual understanding of his wife's position. She was in the car, and she was lost. This represents Soul's journey through the lower worlds as It tries to find Its way home. But until she had at least some idea of where she was, her husband couldn't help her.

All he could do in the dream was encourage her to go very slowly down the road until she came to a crossroad. This gave him the insight to tell her out here, "First you have to find out where you are spiritually. You have to know where you are before you can figure out where to go."

He recommended that she examine her own religion, other spiritual paths, Eckankar, and whatever else she wanted to, but to go very slowly. Eventually she would come to a point in her life that seemed significant.

Then she could stop, take a look around, and see where she was. Tim could then try to help her figure out her direction home.

Create Your Own Dream Dictionary

During important times in my life, one of the dream symbols I used to see was a field with a regular-sized baseball diamond. When everything on the field was aligned and in proper order—four bases evenly spaced, a pitcher, a batter, and two opposing teams—it meant that my life was in good order.

But sometimes the bases were at odd distances apart or the base path wasn't in a perfect square. Or the ball I'd hit might pop and blow feathers all over the place. Or I'd have to run into the woods to find first base. Second base might be closer in than usual; third base might be off in another direction entirely. In other words, everything about the game was wrong.

15

When I'd wake up after a dream like that, I'd often notice that something in my outer life wasn't going right. The sport had gone out of it. There wasn't any fun in it.

This was an indication for me to sit down and work out a plan to reorganize. In other words, I had to figure out how to get myself a real baseball field again— proper space between bases, correct number of players on each team, and so on.

Tip: The Dream Dictionary

Creating a dream dictionary can help you become familiar with your own dream symbols.

Whether a baseball diamond, a bear, an eagle, or anything else, you'll know immediately what a particular symbol means to you.

In a section at the back of your dream journal, keep a list of the symbols that occur in your dreams.

As you create your own dream dictionary of symbols, record the date next to the
meaning of each symbol. This way you can
keep track as the meaning changes. As you
unfold, your dream symbols are going to
take on different meanings, a fact not gen-
erally known by people who study dreams.

Tip: Study the Details

What can you do to remember your
dreams and other inner experiences? You
could write them down, but that's a hard
thing to do. Sometimes you don't feel like
writing. Another way to remember is to
study the details of the experience while
it's happening.

For instance, if you're at a baseball game
in your dream, you could study the uniform
of one of the players on the other team. See
what kind of shoes he's got—cleats or whatever—and what color shirt he has on. Even
notice the stitching on parts of the shirt.

Become aware of the little details. Notice a tree, a cat, and the cat's ears, how he twitches them. This will help you remember your dreams.

Tip: How to Interpret Your Dreams

Remember that dreams have a meaning at the human, emotional, causal, mental, subconscious, and spiritual levels. They correspond to the six planes of existence—the Physical, Astral, Causal, Mental, Etheric, and Soul Planes. Each deals with a part of you, and each of your dreams comes mainly from one of these areas.

Keep the interpretation simple. Look at each dream in one of three levels. Is the dream about your daily life, your emotions and thoughts, or about the pure spiritual side, your relationship with God?

Here, then, are a few tips:

1. Dream—get plenty of rest for a few days. Then go to sleep with the intention

of remembering some of the places you visit while your human self lies sleeping. (It helps to write the dreams down as soon as you awaken.)

2. Interpret your dreams—ask the Dream Master (my inner self) to let you see each dream on three levels: the daily, the emotional/mental, and the spiritual.

3. Realize your dreams—take the dream lessons and apply them to your everyday life.

DREAMS BRING
FREEDOM AND LOVE

*A*s a young girl Danielle liked stories about Peter Pan and Mary Poppins. These characters could fly.

Flying was important for her because she had a little friend she met in her dreams who would come to her house. It was a little Indian boy; he always wore a headband.

They would go off flying together in the Astral body. Sometimes they'd go out just around the yard and play. Then Danielle's sister, in her Astral body, would come out and say, "You come down from there, you two. If you don't come down, I'm going to pound you." Then the little girl and the little boy would fly down just like birds trying to chase someone away. They would do that just to aggravate the older sister. They'd buzz her. That made her angry, and she'd swat at them like pesky flies. They'd keep out of reach, and they'd laugh and laugh up there where the air was rare.

Some of their astral experiences were different. They went on far adventures. When they went on a long trip, the Indian boy brought along his dog, Sam. At times like this they might visit Alaska and other parts of the world. The dog went along to protect them and did very nicely.

Then the kids would come back home again, fly around the neighborhood, and land. Back home, each would then go off to sleep in their astral forms, to wake up later in their own physical bodies. They always remembered these experiences.

As time went on, the experiences became

less and less frequent, until they finally stopped.

Years later, Danielle met a young man who was Indian. She loved the color of his skin, and she loved his hair. She just loved him. Pretty soon they were going steady. Even on their first dates, she felt very comfortable with him. So she said to him, "You remind me of an Indian boy who used to be my very best friend. I used to meet him in dreams."

He said, "You remind me of a little girl I met in my dreams. But she had blond hair. Your hair is brown." She said, "When I was a little kid, my hair was blond."

They began to compare notes. He began to describe what he remembered. "Right near your home, train tracks ran past. I remember your garden," he said. She said, "I remember your headband. You always wore a headband. And your dog's name was Sam."

So they made a connection. They got

married, and now they have two children.

Divine love brought them together from two different races. When their hearts met, their hearts knew. Divine love is that strong.

Sometimes people who will come together later in life are born at literally opposite ends of the earth. But it is not beyond the capacity of the Law of Karma to bring them together. If they're to be together, no force on earth can keep them apart. Love is the tie that binds. Through this love Danielle found her husband, and he found her.

REUNION WITH A
DEPARTED LOVED ONE

*F*ive years had gone by since "Adele's" sister had passed on, or translated. Adele often wondered, *Does my sister still remember me? Why doesn't she come, even in dreams?*

Adele teaches art. She lives in a quiet suburb. One day one of her students looked out and saw a kitten nearby that had apparently been struck by a car. It looked as if it wouldn't be able to live much longer. The student ran outside and tried to catch the little kitten but wasn't able to. For the next week Adele worried about the kitten. She put out food and water because it would need some help in getting fed. But the kitten never showed up.

One Saturday morning, Adele had a very clear dream with her sister. It was a very vivid dream, like they were actually together, because they were. Her sister said to her, "I can take care of the kitten for you if you'll give me some food." So Adele gave her sister a saucer with some food on it.

When Adele awoke, she had this feeling of love. Two concerns were taken from her heart. First of all, the kitten was cared for, probably in the other worlds. And even more important, her sister had not forgotten her. This was a demonstration of divine love.

PRACTICAL
BENEFITS OF DREAMS

$\mathcal{S}$ometimes a lesson derived from the dream state brings a healing.

Healing in Dreams

An ECK initiate, "Helen," went to see her doctor about a certain health problem. He gave her two prescriptions which had proven helpful to other patients with the same condition. She took the medications faithfully for a few days but finally concluded that they were not going to work for her.

One night Helen had a dream—a very simple inner experience. First she saw a plain black screen. Then letters began to appear, one by one, each a different color, spelling out the word *Ornade*. She didn't know exactly what it was, but she had a feeling it was significant for her health. She woke up in the middle of the night and, while the experience was fresh in her mind, she got out of bed and carefully wrote down the word.

The next day Helen called the pharmacist who filled her prescriptions. "Is there a drug called Ornade?" she asked.

"Yes, there is," he said. "It's often used as a decongestant." As far as he knew, it had never been used as a remedy for her particular condition.

A few days later she went to see her doctor again. "The drugs you prescribed don't work for me," she said. "I would like to try Ornade."

"It won't help you at all," he said. "It's perfectly useless for your condition."

Helen felt foolish, but she told him about seeing the name in a dream. She was very persistent about wanting to give it a try, and finally he gave in. "All right," he said. "I don't recommend it, but it won't hurt you."

He wrote her out a prescription. She went directly to the pharmacy to have it filled and began to use the drug that same day. In a short time she found that it worked very well for her, even though it was not intended as a treatment for her condition.

Dreams and Diet

When her eldest son was in sixth grade, "Glenda" found that he was often sick on Monday mornings. The teacher concluded, "He's got school phobia; just send him to school." The doctor said, "Give him these medications, and send him to school." But Glenda wanted to find out what the problem really was.

One night in a dream she got a nudge to begin checking her son's diet.

She recorded what he ate during the week and what he ate on weekends. And she found out he ate more ice cream on the weekends than at any other time.

Glenda experimented. She found that when he didn't have ice cream or other milk products on the weekends, he was fine on Monday, ready to go to school. She concluded that he was sensitive to dairy products.

She could've been intimidated by the school officials, who were highly educated. They huffed and puffed and said, "Send him to school anyway." But she said no; she knew there was something else. Because the still small voice of the Mahanta was speaking to her and nudging her to look a little bit further, she found the food sensitivity.

Spiritual Exercise: How to Heal Yourself

A way to heal oneself begins with a spiritual exercise. At bedtime, sing the word

HU (pronounced like the word *hue*, but long and drawn-out). Softly sing this ancient name for God for five to ten minutes. Also create a mental picture of your problem. See it as a simple cartoon. Beside it, place another image of the condition as you feel it should be.

Keep a record of your dreams. Make a short note about every dream you recall upon awakening. Also be alert during the day for clues about your problem from other people. The Holy Spirit works through them too.

Help in Business

A businessman, "Andrew," had the responsibility of accounting for the funds of small firms. He hadn't kept his books up for a while, and one night he had a dream. In the dream, two young men came into his room and began examining the accounting books. Andrew stood off to the side, watching as the accountants sat down and began to audit the books.

When he woke up in the morning, he immediately started catching up on his ledger accounts, straightening everything out. He worked on this for a couple of mornings, and his wife asked him, "Why are you taking care of the books, when normally you'd be getting ready for work?"

"I don't know," he said. "I just have this strong feeling to do it."

On the third day, Andrew was at work, when two young men walked in the door. They were auditors; they had come to audit his books. And he was ready, all because he had trusted the message he got from his dream.

Dream Help with Finances

In an African country where hyperinflation has taken over, an ECKist, "Peter," and his wife were having a very hard time making ends meet. They didn't know what to do. Some outstanding bills were about to come due, and the family needed money to pay them.

One night in the dream state the Mahanta came to Peter, and in his hand the Mahanta carried a belt. Just a belt. He handed it to the dreamer.

Peter said, "What do you want me to do with this belt?"

The Mahanta said, "Tighten it."

So when they woke up in the morning, Peter and his wife sat down and made a budget. They figured out where they were going to tighten their belts and cut expenses. And because they did this, they were able to cope with the inflation. They had taken measures to do it.

An inner experience can give us an insight into our outer experience. The dream becomes like a play with hidden meaning, which gives us a clue about the outcome of our outer life.

Light and Sound Bring Spiritual Unfoldment

One aspect of the ECK (Holy Spirit) is the Light of God. Some people have experiences with It. Others have experiences with the Sound of God. It all depends upon the line of spiritual unfoldment they have chosen to follow in their past lives upon earth.

Celestial Light

When he was thirteen, "Devon" experienced the Light of God in an unusual way. One particular night a lightning bolt shot past his left shoulder.

The sky was absolutely clear, so he could not understand what might have happened to him. This incident took place about the time that he began searching through books for a truth greater than that of his own religion.

Years passed. One night he and a childhood friend were sitting outside on a car. Suddenly the whole southern horizon lit up as if it were daylight. They both sat stunned for a second, then asked each other, "Did you see that?" The Mahanta was responsible for this experience to further awaken the Spiritual Eye of Soul. No one else in the area reported the unusual phenomenon of celestial light.

By and by, Devon moved to another state and joined the Mormon Church. During his youth he had seen occasional flashes of light, and now they began to return. He was coming closer to the day that he would find Eckankar.

At a church meeting he tried to describe to others the Blue Light he often saw: it was about the size of a quarter and appeared at unexpected intervals. Nobody knew what he was talking about, since the Light of God was not a part of their experience.

About this time Devon had a vivid dream in which Simha, the Lady of ECK, appeared to him. He had just fallen asleep, when he found himself standing before a blond woman. She wore a blue robe and called him her son. She assured him that he was progressing well in his spiritual unfoldment, but he was to continue his search for truth.

What astounded him was the tremendous love he felt in her presence. It was like a wave rolling across the ocean. The wave of love was the Sound Current, which was pouring out to him through the Lady of ECK. That was years ago. Since then, Divine Spirit has brought a change to Devon's life: mainly, fear is fading away. In its stead he is developing a compassionate, yet detached love for all living things.

Dream Music

A man wrote me of the following experience he had in a dream.

"Jeff" said that whenever he was waking up from sleep, he would feel as though he were falling from a great height and as if he were out of the body. He said that he never felt afraid because he felt familiar with the vibrations of those heights. What was most interesting, Jeff said, "was the beautiful music I always heard. Often I heard madrigals, with mostly female voices."

When he was waking up, Soul was coming back to the body from the higher planes. This gives the feeling of falling from a great height and is a Soul Travel experience.

Hearing the madrigal indicates Soul Travel on the Mental Plane, since this form of song particularly develops the Mental body. The madrigal is another expression of the Sound Current there in addition to the sound of running water.

Spiritual Exercise: Golden Musical Notes

Here is a simple exercise to help you experience the Sound of ECK.

Sit or lie down, close your eyes, and place your attention on the Spiritual Eye (a spot behind and between the eyebrows). Chant *HU* (see pages 29–30). As you chant, listen carefully in a gentle way. Use the creative imagination. Try to visualize the Sound as golden musical notes flowing down from a place above you.

As you see them, know that each golden note has an accompanying sound. Listen for the melodies as they pass into and through you in a continuous stream.

Visualize something connected with the music that strikes a definite image on your mind, perhaps a stringed instrument, a flute, or another woodwind. First try to see, then try to hear the golden notes flowing down from this musical instrument.

Know that you are listening to the melody
of God.

Working Consciously
with Sound and Light

The Sound and Light of God are very
real in ECK.

The Light we speak of is the manifesta-
tion of the Holy Spirit at a certain rate of
vibration. It's a rate of vibration in which
the atoms of God can be seen. As these
atoms move faster at a higher level of vibration, they can be heard as the Sound
Current of ECK.

The Light is seen in many different
ways, depending upon the individual's state
of consciousness. It may come as a blue
flash, like flashbulbs going off, or as a blue
globe which looks like a very steady small
blue light. This is known as the Blue Light
of the Mahanta.

Another form is the white light or a
yellowish-white light. Sometimes it looks

like the sun but much more brilliant and pure. It can be seen as a green, lavender, or pink light. Jakob Böhme, the mystic cobbler, saw everything with an aura of pinkness about it, which is one of the preliminary stages of the Light of God. Any of these manifestations simply means that the Light of God is coming to show Soul the way home to the heavenly kingdom, to the Godhead.

The Sound does not come as the voice of an awesome deity speaking to you. Instead, depending upon your level of consciousness during contemplation or in the dream state, It can come in the form of music, the different sounds of nature, or any number of ways.

For instance, you might hear It as the buzzing of insects, the twittering of birds, the tinkling of bells, or musical instruments. What it means is that, at this particular time, the Sound of God is entering into you to bring about the purification of Soul.

Sometimes people have experiences with the Light and Sound before coming to ECK, but they don't know what it all means.

The Light and Sound are actual, definite aspects of the Holy Spirit, understood and achieved through the Spiritual Exercises of ECK. Many of these are given in books such as *The Spiritual Exercises of ECK*. The ECK teachings are built specifically upon these two pillars of God in a direct, knowable way.

Spiritual Guides in Dreams

*T*he ECK Masters sometimes work in the dream state, and sometimes they help more directly, if people are in trouble and need protection when something comes up very quickly.

These Masters are here to help you. When the time is right and you need the help, you will find someone like Rebazar Tarzs, a Tibetan ECK Master, or Paul Twitchell, who founded the modern-day teachings of Eckankar. They will come, and they'll help you.

You may wonder, *Why would these people help me, a stranger?* Sometimes people ask me about this, saying, "After all, I'm a Christian. I don't believe in ECK Masters."

41

But remember that one of the principles in ECK is reincarnation. Nearly 99 percent of the people who come to ECK in this lifetime have been a follower of ECK in the past under one of these ECK Masters.

Sri Harold Klemp   Paul Twitchell   Rebazar Tarzs   Gopal Das

We provide pictures of the ECK Masters for this reason. Some of them are in our books; sometimes we have them available in other ways, like at an ECK center in your area. We do this for those who come to Eckankar for the first time, so that they may recognize one of their dream teachers.

These dream teachers, the ECK Masters, are often with people for their entire lives—long before they've ever heard of Eckankar.

Accepting the Love

A woman from Australia, "Lucinda," had broken up with her fiancé and was going through a very difficult time emotionally. One night she was asleep, when suddenly she got the feeling that someone else was in the room. Opening her eyes, she saw a light that grew brighter and brighter until it filled the entire room. In the center of this light stood a being, the man she later learned was Paul Twitchell.

He came to the side of the bed and, without touching her, held his hands above her. The power of the love of God Lucinda felt in him took away all her fear.

"Who are you?" she asked. "What are you doing here?"

"Be quiet," he answered. "Just accept the love."

And then he was gone.

He came back several more times during those months Lucinda was going through that rough emotional time in her life.

While unpacking boxes in her apartment one day, she came across the book *The Flute of God*, by Paul Twitchell. She couldn't remember ever having bought it. When she saw the author's face on the back cover, she recognized him as the man who had come to her in her dreams. But the book said he had died in 1971. Yet she knew he was alive; he had come and talked with her. That's when she decided to write me to learn more about Eckankar.

A few days later, before she sealed and mailed her letter, Paul Twitchell came to her again, surrounded by light.

He said, "You now have the Light and Sound of God," and he left. After meeting Paul and experiencing the Light of God, she knew that the power of love had more meaning in her life than she had ever realized.

A Dream with Rebazar Tarzs

In the early 1930s, when "Frances" was in the first grade, she had a series of very vivid dreams. She was in a candlelit cavern full of buried bodies. Wolves were growling in the distance, and she could hear them running after her. The dream repeated itself for several nights.

One night the wolves caught up with her, and she called out for help. Instantly two men appeared, one dressed in a maroon robe. The man said, "Turn around, and face them." But Frances was too afraid.

The next night, as she ran through the cavern, Frances noticed that the candles were flickering. They were almost used up. "I'd rather die in the light than in the dark," she said and turned to face the wolves. To her surprise, they vanished. The two men were standing next to her, smiling.

Through the years, Frances continued to have dream experiences with the man in the maroon robe. He emanated such love and kindness that she grew to trust him. As she grew older, he began appearing in her outer life in dramatic ways. Once she saw him save her parents from two men who were trying to kill them. Another time his whispered instructions helped her rescue a cousin who was drowning.

It wasn't until 1940, in her sophomore year of high school, that Frances was able to learn the man's name. It was Rebazar Tarzs.

Still following Catholicism, Frances began meeting with both Jesus and Rebazar in her dreams. One night, Jesus told her that she would begin studying exclusively with Rebazar. When she met Rebazar the next night, she asked him why.

"It's time to move on to higher planes. Jesus teaches up to this region, but it is time to go on." The next night Frances sought out Jesus and asked about what

46

Rebazar had said. He repeated the same thing, saying, "Now return to your Master."

In 1970, when Frances read Paul Twitchell's *ECKANKAR—The Key to Secret Worlds*, she was very surprised to learn that Paul had known Rebazar Tarzs too.

The ECK Masters taught Frances how to face her own fears. As long as you have fear, you will never have true freedom of Soul. This is the whole point of Eckankar: to teach the individual how to reach spiritual freedom and go back to God in this lifetime.

A Dream with Gopal Das

A Japanese woman had recently become an ECKist when she had this dream. "Yuko" was riding on a bus with a few other passengers. She mentioned to the bus driver that she wanted to be let off at a certain stop.

"That's a very dangerous place at night,"

he cautioned her. "You don't want to get off there by yourself."

"I'll go with you," a man on the bus offered.

Yuko and the other passenger got off the bus. They were met by a woman, a child, and one or two other people. Yuko could see the moon in the darkening sky as they walked down the road.

Soon they came to a path that took them to a house high up in the mountains. The man from the bus opened the glass door, and they went inside.

On one wall in this house was a picture of a man with long golden hair. "Who's he?" Yuko asked.

"You remember, don't you?" the man from the bus said.

All of a sudden she did remember: She had come to this mountain home many times before, on that very same bus, accompanied by the man in the picture. The dream ended at that point, but she retained a vivid memory of it.

Shortly after that Yuko attended an ECK Satsang (spiritual study) class. Sketches of four ECK Masters were displayed on a table as part of the class discussion. As she glanced at each one, suddenly her eyes widened in surprise. "That's the man I saw in the picture in my dream!" she said, pointing to one of the sketches. It was the ECK Master Gopal Das.

Meeting the Master Again

A letter came recently. It was addressed to Mr. Klemp and was from someone who is not a member of ECK. "Trudy" went to an Eckankar open house in one of the southern US states. Her husband wanted to go, and she didn't, but she went along anyway. Here are her words:

"When I first went in, I felt like I was among people I knew. I told myself it was because they were so friendly. Then I saw your picture, and I thought, *I've seen him; I know him from somewhere—must be TV or some magazine.*"

While Trudy was at the open house, someone invited her to listen to a tape about HU, the love song to God. "I realized," she writes, "that I had dreamed all of it just a couple of nights before. I'd been there in my dream. I also realized that I knew you from my dreams.

"The first time I saw you, you were on a porch, and you turned to face me as I came up to you. It startled me, for I didn't know you were there until you turned. Our eyes met, and I could tell you meant me no harm. And all my fears left me.

"You said, 'I can help you.' I said, 'No, you can't. No one can.'

"You again told me, 'I can help you.'

"We stood and looked at one another, and I could read you through your eyes. And I was aware that you could read me through mine.

"You told me a third time, 'I can help you. But you must accept it; you must believe me.' You smiled at me, and I thought, *But I know you*. And you said, 'Yes, you know me. But not as who you are now. I've been waiting for you to come to me.'

"And I asked, 'Where did you wait for me?'

"'Where I'm supposed to wait. You lost your way, but I knew you'd find it.'

"And I said, 'I almost know who you are. By what name are you called?' And as I tried to remember it, I woke up."

Dream Master Visit

The Inner Master came to Trudy again in another dream. She writes, "I was in a garden somewhere, and suddenly you were there, and you said, 'See, I found you.' And we both began to laugh, and I woke up laughing. But I remembered your face; it was the same face in the photograph at the open house today.

"I'll probably never meet you in person. I'm writing you this just to share the experience I had with you in my dreams."

Trudy goes on to say that she and her husband probably won't become members because her husband doesn't have the ability to visualize. A lot of times if a mate isn't ready, the other person says, "My mate's not ready, but I know about you, and we can meet in the dream state."

I get these letters, but I don't often share them because it sounds immodest. And it probably is, highly so. I can't help it. If I don't tell you about this, who's going to? I'm simply doing it to give instances of the power of Divine Spirit working through the teachings of ECK, which are alive and dynamic, such as you won't find anywhere else on earth. This is a very direct path to God.

A Spiritual Exercise
to Meet the Mahanta

In contemplation or before sleep, see yourself strolling on a beach. Sing *Harji*, *Wah Z*, or simply *Z* (see glossary, page 85, for pronunciations and more about these names for the Mahanta).

Ahead of you on the sand is a blanket laden with fruit. The Inner Master, the Mahanta, awaits you there. He is always looking for his beloved follower to come in the Soul form. In his hands he cradles a goblet made of precious jewels. He offers it to you.

"In it is the water of life," he says. "Take it and drink."

The water of life is in fact the ECK, the Light and Sound of God. Drink all of It. Visualize the Light and Sound acting gently upon you. Once you drink of this cup, you will never again thirst for a lesser drink. You will always want these pure waters of heaven.

RESEARCHING
PAST LIVES VIA DREAMS

*I*n the dream teachings of ECK, we learn to identify the problems that are plaguing us. The Inner Master begins to open up small scenes from our past. We sometimes perceive these as disjointed dreams. These dream experiences give us a way to start finding out who and what we are.

Dream Insight for Our Lives Today

As we move into the higher states of consciousness, we become more aware of our responsibility—first of all to ourselves, but also to other people. Our responsibility to others is mainly to allow them the same freedom we want for ourselves.

The experiences you have in dreams are to give you another perspective on your life today.

People occasionally have a dream about a past life with another person. Misunderstanding its purpose, they may use it to try to put a hold on that person, who has no recollection of the mutual past life. It becomes a control factor.

When the Dream Master shows you a karmic picture from a past life, it is mainly to give you an insight into yourself as you are today—the most perfect spiritual being you have ever been in all your lives. That is who you are today.

By the same token, if the Dream Master gives you an experience about a future event, the aspect about the future is secondary. Again, it is really about today. If you keep this in mind, you will interpret the experience in a way that will give you more perspective about your present life and how you can live it better.

Tools for Unfoldment

Many Christians believe that life begins at birth—as if the creation of Soul takes place at the birth of the human body—and ends at death, and then continues in heaven.

In the teachings of ECK we learn, sometimes through past-life experiences in the dream state, that we have lived more than just one life. We have lived thousands of lives.

In each life we gather talents, tools, and lessons which help in our spiritual unfoldment in subsequent lifetimes, including this one. Christianity's arena is limited to this one physical lifetime; in ECK we gain a broader vision. We recognize that Soul enters many different bodies throughout Its journey in the lower worlds.

The ECKist learns that the reason he is reborn again and again is to learn how to love, to overcome those traits which prevent him or her from becoming a Co-worker with

God. In each life we learn a little bit more. There is, of course, the grace of God which brings us to the Light and Sound and to the Mahanta; but at the same time, there is just as much effort required on our part.

Exploring Forgotten Worlds

Soon after learning of Soul Travel, I dreamed of a past life in about 10,000 BC, after the last of that all-but-forgotten continent of Lemuria had succumbed to earthquakes and volcanoes, and had sunk into the Pacific. My reincarnation was a century after the final disaster, and my hunting range was on the West Coast of America, in what is today southern California. This dream explained my strong urge in the early 1970s to move back to the same area. The rolling hills of Laguna Beach, California, awoke pleasant memories of the gentle terrain of lost Lemuria. But Lemuria's hot and muggy climate had been host to gigantic insects, which were a decided nuisance.

The dream was of me as a simple wanderer who walked along the edges of a great marsh. Most of North America was yet swampland, except for chains of islands that reached south to the firmer soil of Mexico, and to Central and South America. Dressed in light skins, the wanderer looked to gather wild rice from the marsh, but he needed a boat or a crude raft for the harvesting. While he made a search along the shoreline for driftwood to build a raft, two savage animals, like wild dogs, bounded toward him, intending him for a meal.

Springing into the low branches of a tree, he straddled a limb, his feet safely out of reach of their snapping teeth. The wild animals settled down at the base of the tree, content to wait for him. Studying his plight, the man broke off a sturdy branch and fashioned a club. He dropped to the ground between the savage dogs. They attacked him, and he killed them with vicious blows.

The threat to his life ended, he skinned one of the animals with a sharp stone knife and ate the meat by his campfire. All the time he studied the wild rice in the nearby marsh, planning a way to harvest it. Rice was handy food on a journey, for a traveler could chew a little of it and swallow the juice for nourishment.

This rather commonplace memory of a past life was nonetheless exciting for me. The Spiritual Exercises of ECK had unlocked the Causal Plane records; the Inner Master was letting me have experiences at a rate I could handle.

While we, the actors, polish away the flaws in our spiritual roles, the ages roll on like a slow, deep river—purifying Soul.

Tip: On Past-Life Study

To awaken past-life dreams, make a note of what things you greatly like or dislike. Do that also with people. Then watch your dreams. Also note if a certain country or century attracts you.

There is a reason.

Prophetic Dreams

*N*early all of his life, a man from Ghana has had a recurring dream to show him coming fortune. In the dream, he is always crossing a flooding river: The bigger the flooding, the greater his wealth. Recently, such a prophetic dream revealed that he would gain a certain large sum of money. Soon after that he did, almost to the exact amount.

A woman from Washington State has universally prophetic dreams. Such dreams go beyond the personal life of the dreamer and take in world events.

In one of her dreams, she foresaw the volcanic explosion of Mount Saint Helens three years before it occurred in May 1980.

In another, she witnessed the destructive earthquake in San Francisco a few years before it happened in October 1989. She does not pursue these dreams; they just come. They warn her to steer clear of the immediate areas of danger.

Above the Time Track

There really is no separate past, no separate present, and no separate future. We talk about them as such: we look at past lives that we have spent in some other time, we speak of different things we've experienced. We speak of all that as in the past. But past, present, and future are really one.

We just see things sequentially because the mind is constructed to see things in a linear fashion, along a straight line.

But people who have a particular talent in dreaming or prophecy can get off this linear Time Track. They can get above it in the Soul body. And they can see the past, the present, and the future all in the present moment because they are above time and space.

One of the preliminary steps to coming to this spiritual ability, this spiritual state of consciousness, is dream study. This is why we put so much emphasis on dreams in Eckankar.

Dreams can help you in your daily life. They can help you see what's coming; they can help you see why things are as they are. You'll find you were a key player in the circumstances that brought the situations you find yourself in today.

QUESTIONS AND ANSWERS

*A*s spiritual leader of Eckankar, I get thousands of letters from seekers of truth around the world. All want direct and useful answers about how to travel the road to God. I reply personally to many of these letters.

Here are several questions I've been asked about dreams.

Read on for clues that might help you.

Bad Dreams

Why do some people have bad dreams?

Your question is one that bothers many people today. So let's have a look at it.

First on the list of reasons for bad dreams are frightening TV shows and violent computer games. Especially in the evening before bedtime. One who indulges in them is falling into a lower state of consciousness.

And where do you suppose he dream travels? To the lower Astral Plane. So, do pleasant things before bedtime. It will clear up many bad dreams.

Second, bad dreams may come from poor nutrition. This can be from not eating the right foods or eating the wrong ones. Too much sugar is a problem, but so are preservatives in food, and additives like monosodium glutamate (MSG). It's used in Chinese food and much else. Such additives, sugar, and preservatives fray our nerves. So let's avoid them.

Third, toxins around us can also cause bad dreams. Two common ones are mercury and lead.

The biggest source of mercury pollution comes in communities that burn coal to produce electricity. The burning causes mercury to get into the air, and there's no way to avoid it. Some seafoods, too, are a source of mercury. Ours is a polluted planet, but we all do the best we can.

Toxins are hard to remove from our bodies. There are often doctors of alternative medicine in larger communities who can help us.

So start with reason number one. If you do your part, it'll be easier for me to help you enjoy more pleasant sleep. And sweet dreams!

Real People?

People in my dreams never act the way they do in real life. Why? Am I really with that person on the inner, or not? When I dream of other people, is it about them or what they represent to me? How can I distinguish between the two? How do I find a balance between the dream world and my physical life? If I have a disturbing dream about someone, how can I understand the spiritual gift and then let it go?

You really are with that person on the inner. But a couple of things come into play.

First, you may not remember the inner experience exactly as it happened. The dream censor, which is part of the subconscious mind, is responsible for that. It represents the social part of the Kal, the negative force. His reason is that you're not ready to handle the truth—which may be true. So your recall is clouded. That's illusion. It protects you from emotional shocks.

Second, your distorted recall of the dream will *represent* a hidden truth, instead of giving the actual truth face-to-face. So you must decipher it by asking the Mahanta, the Inner Master, for help in understanding. Ask him for help during contemplation.

Every well-balanced person finds a balance between the dream world and the physical life.

Remember, the physical laws are for the physical world, while the laws of the dream world are for the dream world. Keep them separate. Unless you do, you're likely to blunder into some terrible mistakes.

For example, let's say someone in your dream expresses ardent love for you. You take that for his true feelings in the physical world. He may not be aware of them yet and will consider your sudden friendliness pushy. He'll back right off, afraid of you. Actually he's afraid of something he wasn't prepared for—your love.

In this case, play it cool. Feel out the situation a little at a time. Test the waters. Also be ready to accept the fact that this relationship will never develop. Here again, the realities of the dream world may not be suitable for the physical world.

Study your dreams. You'll learn what your dreams mean to your physical life with the Mahanta's help. You keep in touch with him by doing the Spiritual Exercises of ECK.

The Gentle Way of Dreaming

I am having difficulty with my dreams because I cannot stop worrying over details of my physical life. Please, I need your help.

Put forth every effort to learn and grow during the lessons of the day with a light attention on the presence of the Spirit of God.

The point is: Carry out the physical duties and responsibilities as if you're doing them for God.

Do the Spiritual Exercises of ECK as you usually do them, but at bedtime give a thought request to the Mahanta, with love and goodwill in the heart center: *I give you permission to take me to wherever you see I've earned the right.* Then go peacefully to sleep without giving all this another thought.

You can vary the phrasing every few weeks for the benefit of the mind, which likes the stimulation of new ideas.

Sometimes we try too hard and push

against the doors of Soul, forgetting that the doors open inwardly and cannot be forced. The spiritual exercises work best if one can fill himself with love and goodwill by thinking of someone who makes him happy.

This gentle technique can bring one to a conscious awakening in the dream state.

THE ANCIENT
PROMISE RENEWED

*I*f the dream teachings of ECK achieve anything, may it be to show people how the Holy Spirit teaches through both Its inner and outer guidance. This lifetime is our spiritual laboratory.

We lay out our spiritual chemistry kit on a table and make experiments in our lives regarding the far-reaching, but often unseen and unknown, laws of life. Experience alone lets us determine what is good for us or not.

Whoever seeks God with a pure heart shall find Him. This promise of the ancient ECK Masters is renewed today.

71

We learn first by dreams. Then, by one of the many aspects of Soul Travel, whether it includes the fantastic out-of-the-body experience or something more subtle. After that comes our first important spiritual realization, which is from the Soul Plane. And finally, if Soul desires God badly enough, It enters God Consciousness.

The most direct, yet most fulfilling, path to the Kingdom of God is still love. It is the beginning and ending of all things.

The path of ECK, then, provides the way for us to receive the joy of God into our hearts and lives. Even so, we must return this holy love to all life. No matter how far we venture into the uncharted reaches of God, we find it to be the endless journey.

Next Steps in Spiritual Exploration

- **Try a spiritual exercise.**
  Review the spiritual exercises in this book or on our Web site.
  Experiment with them.

- **Browse our Web site: www.Eckankar.org.**
  Watch videos; get free books, answers to FAQs, and more info.

- **Attend an Eckankar event in your area.**
  Visit "Eckankar around the World" on our Web site.

- **Read additional books** about the ECK teachings.

- **Explore advanced spiritual study** with the Eckankar discourses that come with membership.

- **Call or write to us:** Call 1-800-LOVE GOD (1-800-568-3463, toll-free, automated) or (952) 380-2200 (direct).

- Write to: ECKANKAR, Dept. BK103, PO Box 2000, Chanhassen, MN 55317-2000 USA.

For Further Reading
By Harold Klemp

ECK Wisdom on Conquering Fear

Would having more courage and confidence help you make the most of this lifetime?

Going far beyond typical self-help advice, this book invites you to explore divine love as the antidote to anxiety and the doorway to inner freedom.

You will discover ways to identify the karmic roots of fear and align with your highest ideals.

Use this book to soar beyond your limitations and reap the benefits of self-mastery.

Live life to its fullest potential!

Spiritual Wisdom on Health and Healing

This booklet is rich with spiritual keys to better health on every level.

Discover the spiritual roots of illness and how gratitude can open your heart to God's love and healing.

Simple spiritual exercises go deep to help you get personal divine guidance and insights.

Revitalize your connection with the true healing power of God's love.

ECK Wisdom on Inner Guidance

Looking for answers, guidance, protection?

Help can come as a nudge, a dream, a vision, or a quiet voice within you. This book offers new ways to connect with the ever-present guidance of ECK, the Holy Spirit. Start today!

Discover how to listen to the Voice of God; attune to your true self; work with an inner guide; benefit from dreams, waking dreams, and Golden-tongued Wisdom; and ignite your creativity to solve problems.

Each story, technique, and spiritual exercise is a doorway to greater confidence and love for life.

Open your heart and let God's voice speak to you!

ECK Wisdom on Karma and Reincarnation

Have you lived before? What is the real meaning of life?

Discover your divine destiny—to move beyond the limits of karma and reincarnation and gain spiritual freedom.

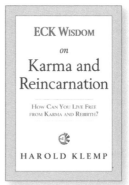

This book reveals the purpose of living and the keys to spiritual growth.

You'll find answers to age-old questions about fate, destiny, and free will. These gems of wisdom can enhance your relationships, health, and happiness—and offer the chance to resolve all your karma in this lifetime!

ECK Wisdom on Life after Death

All that lies ahead is already within your heart.

ECK Wisdom on Life after Death invites you to explore the eternal nature of you!

Author Harold Klemp offers you new perspectives on seeing heaven before you die, meeting with departed loved ones, near-death experiences, getting help from spiritual guides, animals in heaven, and dealing with grief.

Try the techniques and spiritual exercise included in this book to find answers and explore the secrets of life after death—for yourself.

Spiritual Wisdom on Prayer, Meditation, and Contemplation

Bring balance and wonder to your life!

This booklet is a portal to your direct, personal connection with Divine Spirit.

Harold Klemp shows how you can experience the powerful benefits of contemplation—"a conversation with the most secret, most genuine, and most mysterious part of yourself."

Move beyond traditional meditation via dynamic spiritual exercises. Learn about the uplifting chant of HU (an ancient holy name for God), visualization, creative imagination, and other active techniques.

Spiritual Wisdom on Relationships

Find the answers to common questions of the heart, including the truth about Soul mates, how to strengthen a marriage, and how to know if a partnership is worth developing.

The spiritual exercises included in this booklet can help you break a pattern of poor relationships and find balance. You'll learn new ways to open your heart to love and enrich your relationship with God.

This booklet is a key for anyone wanting more love to give, more love to get. It's a key to better relationships with everyone in your life.

ECK Wisdom on Solving Problems

Problems? Problems! Why do we have so many? What causes them? Can we avoid them?

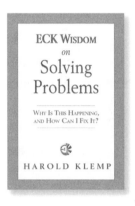

Author Harold Klemp, the spiritual leader of Eckankar, can help you answer these questions and more. His sense of humor and practical approach offer spiritual keys to unlock the secrets to effective problem solving. Learn creative, time-tested techniques to

- Find the root cause of a problem
- Change your viewpoint and overcome difficulties
- Conquer your fears
- Work beyond symptoms to solutions
- Kindle your creativity
- Master your karma, past and present
- Receive spiritual guidance that can transform the way you see yourself and your life

The Call of Soul

Discover how to find spiritual freedom in this lifetime and the infinite world of God's love for you. Includes a CD with dream and Soul Travel techniques.

HU, the Most Beautiful Prayer

Singing *HU*, the ancient name for God, can open your heart and lead you to a new understanding of yourself. Includes a CD of the HU song.

Past Lives, Dreams, and Soul Travel

These stories and exercises help you find your true purpose, discover greater love than you've ever known, and learn that spiritual freedom is within reach.

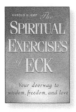

The Spiritual Exercises of ECK

This book is a staircase with 131 steps leading to the doorway to spiritual freedom, self-mastery, wisdom, and love. A comprehensive volume of spiritual exercises for every need.

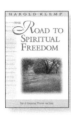

The Road to Spiritual Freedom, Mahanta Transcripts, Book 17

Sri Harold's wisdom and heart-opening stories of everyday people having extraordinary experiences tell of a secret truth at work in *your* life—there is divine purpose and meaning to every experience you have.

How to Survive Spiritually in Our Times, Mahanta Transcripts, Book 16

Discover how to reinvent yourself spiritually—to thrive in a changing world. Stories, tools, techniques, and spiritual insights to apply in your life now.

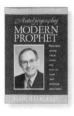

Autobiography of a Modern Prophet

This riveting story of Harold Klemp's climb up the Mountain of God will help you discover the keys to your own spiritual greatness.

Those Wonderful ECK Masters

Would you like to have *personal* experience with spiritual masters that people all over the world—since the beginning of time—have looked to for guidance, protection, and divine love? This book includes real-life stories and spiritual exercises to meet eleven ECK Masters.

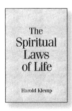

The Spiritual Laws of Life

Learn how to keep in tune with your true spiritual nature. Spiritual laws reveal the behind-the-scenes forces at work in your daily life.

Available at bookstores, from online booksellers, or directly from Eckankar: www.ECKBooks.org; (952) 380-2200; ECKANKAR, Dept. BK103, PO Box 2000, Chanhassen, MN 55317-2000 USA.

GLOSSARY

Words set in SMALL CAPS are defined elsewhere in this glossary.

Blue Light   How the MAHANTA often appears in the inner worlds to the CHELA or seeker.

chela   A spiritual student. Often a member of ECKANKAR.

ECK   The Life Force, the Holy Spirit, or Audible Life Current which sustains all life.

Eckankar *EHK-ahn-kahr*   The Path of Spiritual Freedom. Also known as the Ancient Science of SOUL TRAVEL. A truly spiritual way of life for the individual in modern times. The teachings provide a framework for anyone to explore their own spiritual experiences. Established by PAUL TWITCHELL, the modern-day founder, in 1965. The word means Co-worker with God.

ECK Masters   Spiritual Masters who can assist and protect people in their spiritual studies and travels. The ECK Masters are from a long line of God-Realized SOULS who know the responsibility that goes with spiritual freedom.

God-Realization   The state of God Consciousness. Complete and conscious awareness of God.

Gopal Das *GHO-pahl DAHS* The guardian of the SHARIYAT-KI-SUGMAD at the Temple of Askleposis on the Astral PLANE. He was the MAHANTA, the LIVING ECK MASTER in Egypt, about 3000 BC.

Harji *HAYR-jee* A respectful name of affection for SRI Harold Klemp. *See also* KLEMP, HAROLD; WAH Z; Z.

HU *HYOO* The most ancient, secret name for God. The singing of the word *HU* is considered a love song to God. It can be sung aloud or silently to oneself to align with God's love.

initiation Earned by a member of ECKANKAR through spiritual unfoldment and service to God. The initiation is a private ceremony in which the individual is linked to the Sound and Light of God.

Kal Niranjan *KAL nee-RAHN-jahn* The Kal; the negative power, also known as Satan or the devil.

Karma, Law of The Law of Cause and Effect, action and reaction, justice, retribution, and reward, which applies to the lower or psychic worlds: the Physical, Astral, Causal, Mental, and Etheric PLANES.

Klemp, Harold The present MAHANTA, the LIVING ECK MASTER. SRI Harold Klemp became the Mahanta, the Living ECK Master in 1981. His spiritual name is WAH Z.

Living ECK Master The title of the spiritual leader of ECKANKAR. He leads SOUL back to God. He teaches in the physical world as the Outer Master, in the dream state as the Dream Master, and in the spiritual worlds as the Inner Master. SRI HAROLD KLEMP became the MAHANTA, the Living ECK Master in 1981.

Mahanta An expression of the Spirit of God that is always with you. Sometimes seen as a BLUE LIGHT or Blue Star or in the form of the Mahanta, the LIVING ECK MASTER. The highest state of God Consciousness on earth, only embodied in the Living ECK Master. He is the Living Word.

Peddar Zaskq The spiritual name for PAUL TWITCHELL, the modern-day founder of ECKANKAR and the MAHANTA, the LIVING ECK MASTER from 1965 to 1971.

planes Levels of existence, such as the Physical, Astral, Causal, Mental, Etheric, and SOUL Planes.

Rebazar Tarzs A Tibetan ECK MASTER known as the Torchbearer of ECKANKAR in the lower worlds.

Satsang A class in which students of ECK study a monthly lesson from ECKANKAR.

Self-Realization SOUL recognition. The entering of Soul into the Soul PLANE and there beholding Itself as pure Spirit. A state of seeing, knowing, and being.

Shariyat-Ki-Sugmad The sacred scriptures of ECKANKAR. The scriptures are comprised of twelve volumes in the spiritual worlds. The first two were transcribed from the inner PLANES by PAUL TWITCHELL, modern-day founder of Eckankar.

Soul The True Self, an individual, eternal spark of God. The inner, most sacred part of each person. Soul can see, know, and perceive all things. It is the creative center of Its own world.

Soul Travel The expansion of consciousness. The ability of SOUL to transcend the physical body and travel into the spiritual worlds of God. Soul Travel is taught only by the LIVING ECK MASTER. It helps people unfold spiritually and can provide proof of the existence of God and life after death.

Sound and Light of ECK The Holy Spirit. The two aspects through which God appears in the lower worlds. People can experience them by looking and listening within themselves and through SOUL TRAVEL.

Spiritual Exercises of ECK Daily practices for direct, personal experiences with the Sound Current. Creative techniques using contemplation and the singing of sacred words to bring the higher awareness of SOUL into daily life.

Sri *SREE* A title of spiritual respect, similar to reverend or pastor, used for those who have attained the Kingdom of God. In ECKANKAR, it is reserved for the MAHANTA, the LIVING ECK MASTER.

Sugmad *SOOG-mahd* A sacred name for God. It is the source of all life, neither male nor female, the Ocean of Love and Mercy.

Temple(s) of Golden Wisdom These Golden Wisdom Temples found on the various PLANES— from the Physical to the Anami Lok; CHELAS of ECKANKAR are taken to these temples in the SOUL body to be educated in the divine knowledge; sections of the SHARIYAT-KI-SUGMAD, the sacred teachings of ECK, are kept at these temples.

Twitchell, Paul An American ECK MASTER who brought the modern teachings of ECKANKAR to the world through his writings and lectures. His spiritual name is PEDDAR ZASKQ.

Wah Z *WAH zee* The spiritual name of SRI HAROLD KLEMP. It means the Secret Doctrine. It is his name in the spiritual worlds.

Z Spiritual name for SRI HAROLD KLEMP. See also WAH Z.

For more explanations of ECKANKAR terms, see *A Cosmic Sea of Words: The ECKANKAR Lexicon* by Harold Klemp.

About the Author

Author Harold Klemp is known as a pioneer of today's focus on "everyday spirituality." He was raised on a Wisconsin farm and attended divinity school. He also served in the US Air Force.

In 1981, after lifetimes of training, he became the spiritual leader of Eckankar, the Path of Spiritual Freedom. His full title is Sri Harold Klemp, the Mahanta, the Living ECK Master. His mission is to help people find their way back to God in this life.

Each year, Harold Klemp speaks to many thousands of seekers at Eckankar seminars. Author of more than one hundred books, he continues to write, including many articles and spiritual-study discourses. His inspiring and practical approach to spirituality helps many thousands of people worldwide find greater freedom, wisdom, and love in their lives.